Can you see the Moon right now?

CURIOUS
Questions & answers about...
The Moon

If you were a spacecraft, where would you go?

Would you rather be an astronomer or an astronaut?

What would you say if you met an alien on the Moon?

Who's your best friend?

Words by Anne Rooney

Illustrations by Ana Gomez

Miles Kelly

What is a moon?

A moon is a rocky body that orbits (moves around) a bigger object. Most planets in our Solar System have moons. Earth has one, which we simply call 'the Moon'.

> I'm an artificial satellite, put into space by humans.

> Anything that orbits a planet regularly is called a satellite. I'm a natural satellite.

Moon's orbit

The Moon

Axis →

Direction of the Moon's spin

How big is our Moon?

The Moon is small enough that it would fit inside Earth fifty times over. It's still the fifth biggest moon in the Solar System, though!

Does the Moon move?

It orbits Earth, and it moves with Earth around the Sun. The Moon also spins, turning on its axis (an imaginary line through the centre). It takes the same amount of time to turn once on its axis as to orbit Earth once (about 28 days).

The Moon   *Distance between Earth and the Moon, to scale*

The Moon is kept in orbit by gravity, a force that draws objects with mass towards each other. The pull of my gravity keeps the Moon from escaping into space.

Earth

Axis

Direction of Earth's spin

Is it far away?

Pretty far! The Moon is about 384,400 kilometres away from Earth. But it doesn't travel in a perfect circle, so sometimes it's a bit further away and sometimes a bit closer.

= 10,000 kilometres

Earth

Where did the Moon come from?

It formed 4.5 billion years ago, when Earth was very new.

Early Earth

Theia

WHiZZ!

① A planet about the size of Mars, which has been named Theia, smashed into Earth.

② The energy of the crash melted a large amount of rocky Earth and Theia, and mixed them together.

CRASH!

3   Some of the molten (liquid) rock fell back to Earth and became part of our planet, but some was thrown out into space. It cooled, turning back into hard rock.

4   The bits of rock whizzed around Earth, bumping into each other. Eventually, all the lumps pulled together and fused...

...making me!

What's inside the Moon?

Mostly rock. In the centre, there is a small core made of metal, mostly iron. It's surrounded by a layer of hot, semi-molten metal.

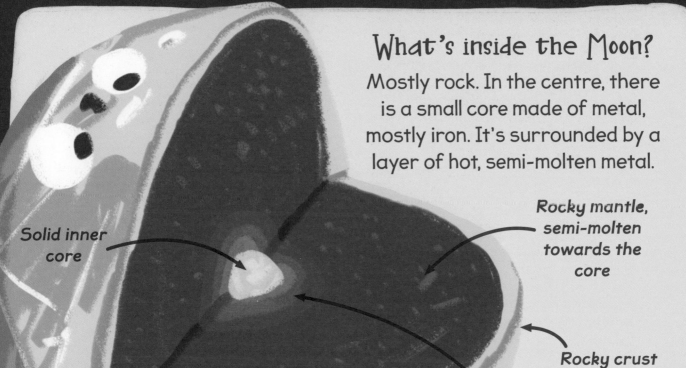

Solid inner core

Rocky mantle, semi-molten towards the core

Rocky crust

Semi-molten outer core

Are there mountains on the Moon?

Yes! The Moon's landscape is made up of mountains, craters and flat plains. The surface is rocky, covered with a deep layer of dust called regolith.

Is it hot or cold?

Both! It's scorching in the daytime when the Moon faces the Sun – it can be 127° Celsius. But it gets down to –173° Celsius at night. Daytime and nighttime each last about two weeks, so any spot has lots of time to get hot or cold.

How can you jump so high?

Gravity is much weaker on the Moon, so people can jump easily and don't fall as quickly. A human can jump about 3 metres high and stay up for around 4 seconds.

Can you see the Sun and stars?

You can see the Sun in the daytime and the stars at night, just as you can on Earth. In daytime, the Sun is too bright for the stars to be visible. At night, the stars are dim as light reflected from Earth makes them hard to see.

You can also see Earth from the Moon, as long as you stand on the side facing Earth! It doesn't move across the Moon's sky, it hangs in one place all the time.

How many?

Regolith on the Moon's surface is **2-8** metres deep.

On the Moon, there are **500 million** craters that are more than 10 metres across.

It took Apollo 11 **51** hours **49** minutes to reach the Moon.

214

The number of known planetary moons in the Solar System.

12

The number of astronauts who have stood on the Moon.

1737 The diameter (distance across) of the Moon in kilometres.

Neil Armstrong spent a total of **2** hours **12** minutes on the Moon's surface (outside the lander).

Eugene Cernan of Apollo 17 spent the longest time outside the lander, a total of **22** hours **5** minutes.

The Apollo 17 Moon buggy was driven the furthest, over **35** kilometres.

$25.8 billion The cost of the whole Apollo program ($194.3 billion at today's prices).

The Moon's gravity is **1/6** of Earth's gravity.

Ganymede

5268

The diameter in kilometres of the largest moon in the Solar System, Jupiter's moon Ganymede — it's bigger than the planet Mercury!

Mercury

The Apollo missions brought back **382** kilograms of Moon rock.

Why do we only see one side of the Moon?

The Moon takes as long to turn once on its axis as it takes to orbit Earth. This means the same side of the Moon is always facing us – this is called tidal locking.

Far side

Near side

North Pole

Near side

Sea of Showers

Copernicus Crater

Sea of Serenity

Ocean of Storms

Sea of Tranquility

Sea of Fertility

Tycho Crater

The dark patches are plains that were once covered by floods of molten rock. They're called seas, even though there's no water!

What is the far side like?

It's very different from the near side. The far side has many more small craters, and even craters within the craters. It has very few flat plains, and its colouring is more irregular.

Has anyone seen the far side?

It can only be seen in photos and from space. It was first seen by humans in 1968, when the Apollo 8 spacecraft went round the Moon. A Chinese spacecraft, Chang'e 4, landed on the far side in 2019 and took the first ground-based photos.

The huge South Pole-Aitken Basin stretches across almost a quarter of the Moon. Basins are massive impact craters.

Far side

Birkhoff Crater

Sea of Moscow

Hertzsprung Crater

Mendeleev Crater

Eastern Sea

Gagarin Crater

South Pole-Aitken Basin

What is a crater?

A crater is a round dent with sloping sides. The Moon is covered in craters. They are caused by meteors crashing into the surface and gouging out holes.

We've been causing craters for billions of years, on the Moon as well as on planets and other moons.

① A meteor speeds towards the Moon.

② The impact causes a shockwave, which blasts a hole in the surface.

③ Moon rock pushed out of the way is forced upwards. The meteor is destroyed.

④ Bits of smashed rock fall nearby, adding a slope to the rim of the crater.

Do meteors hit both sides of the Moon?

Yes, but the near side has far fewer craters. The near side's surface is much thinner, so meteor impacts long ago broke through it. Hot, liquid rock (magma) from inside the Moon flooded out and hardened, smoothing the craters and forming the plains.

The surface on the far side is too thick to break, so its craters never healed.

Will the craters ever disappear?

The Moon doesn't have wind or flowing water, so there is nothing to get rid of the craters. Once the inside of the Moon cooled, craters could no longer be filled in by magma.

When meteors hit Earth, they usually burn up in the atmosphere. The Moon has no atmosphere, so meteors crash into the surface.

Did you know?

The Chang'e 4 spacecraft grew the first plant on the Moon — a **cotton plant** — inside a special container. It survived for 14 Earth days.

An explosion during the flight of **Apollo 13** damaged the spacecraft, so the crew had to loop around the Moon and return without landing.

There are **moonquakes** (like earthquakes). Some are caused by Earth's gravity pulling at the Moon's insides.

Many spacecraft have orbited or landed on the Moon since I did!

The first spacecraft to land on the Moon was the Soviet craft **Luna 2** on 13 September, 1959. It crashed into the surface (on purpose!).

Footprints on the Moon will stay there unless disturbed. They are just slowly worn away by meteoric dust hitting the Moon.

As far as we can tell, **nothing** has ever lived on the Moon.

The Moon is slowly moving further from Earth, at a rate of about **4 centimetres** a year.

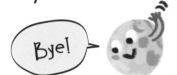

Bye!

Apollo 15 astronaut David Scott dropped a **hammer** and a **feather** on the Moon to show they both fall at the same speed when there is no air.

We were left behind to save weight for the return journey.

The 12 **full moons** of the year have names: wolf, snow, worm, pink, flower, strawberry, buck, sturgeon, harvest, hunter's, beaver and cold moons.

Astronauts left all their **personal waste** in bags on the Moon – and lots of other rubbish and bits of spacecraft.

Hoooooow!!

SERPENT SEA

The Moon's **plains** have names such as Sea of Cleverness, Serpent Sea and Sea of Waves.

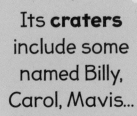

Its **craters** include some named Billy, Carol, Mavis...

...and Bruce!

This is how my phases look from Earth!

New Moon

Waxing Crescent

First Quarter

Waxing Gibbous

Does the Moon change shape?

It seems to change shape, but it doesn't really. As it moves around Earth, different parts are lit by the Sun. The changes are called phases.

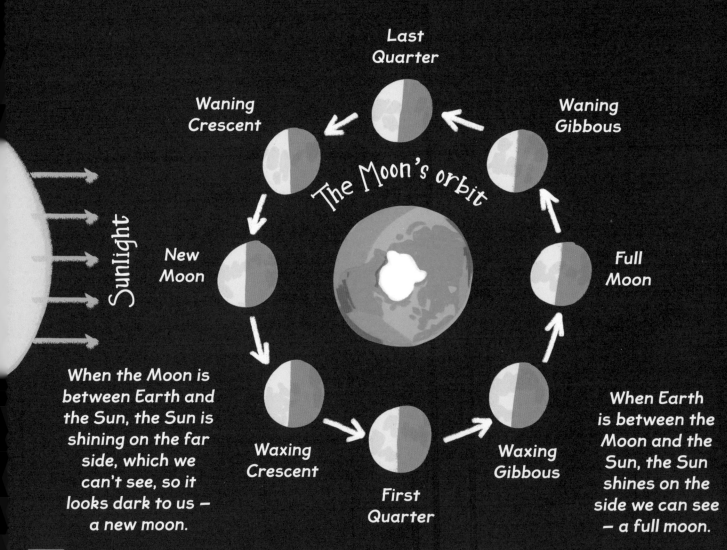

Last Quarter

Waning Crescent

Waning Gibbous

Sunlight

The Moon's orbit

New Moon

Full Moon

Waxing Crescent

First Quarter

Waxing Gibbous

When the Moon is between Earth and the Sun, the Sun is shining on the far side, which we can't see, so it looks dark to us – a new moon.

When Earth is between the Moon and the Sun, the Sun shines on the side we can see – a full moon.

Full Moon

Waning Gibbous

Last Quarter

Waning Crescent

i seem to shine because i reflect the sunlight that falls on me. i don't make my own light, like the Sun or other stars.

Why is the Moon sometimes red?

During a total lunar eclipse, the Sun is directly behind Earth and so the Moon is in Earth's shadow. Some of the sunlight passing through Earth's atmosphere is bent towards the Moon, turning it red.

Total solar eclipse

Can the Moon block out the Sun?

Yes – during a solar eclipse. When the Moon moves between Earth and the Sun and they line up exactly, the Moon's shadow moves over Earth. In some places, it blocks out the Sun completely for a few minutes – a total eclipse.

During a total solar eclipse, parts of Earth are plunged into darkness.

How does the Moon move the sea?

The Moon's gravity pulls at Earth's oceans. This makes the water pile up on the side nearest the Moon, creating a bulge. The water also piles up to make a bulge on the other side.

It's high tide here!

The bulge sweeps round Earth, pulled along by the Moon's gravity as it orbits, and also by Earth turning underneath. This creates the tides.

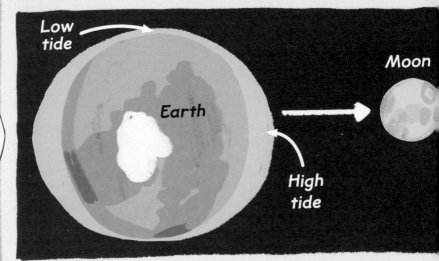

Low tide

Earth

Moon

High tide

Most coasts have two high tides a day, one when nearest the Moon and one when furthest from it.

What causes very high and low tides?

The Sun also helps make the tides. When the Sun and Moon are lined up (at full moon and new moon), they pull in the same direction. This creates extra-high and low tides, called spring tides.

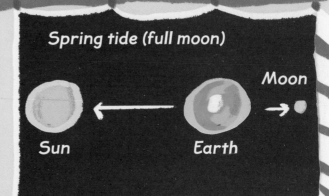

Spring tide (full moon)

Sun

Earth

Moon

Now it's low tide!

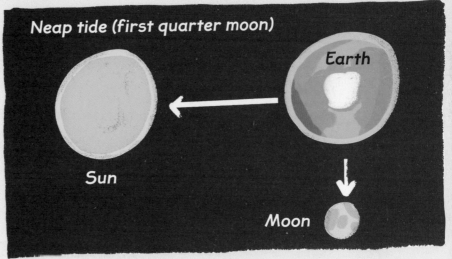

Neap tide (first quarter moon)

Earth

Sun

Moon

When the Sun and Moon are at right angles to each other, there are smaller tides than usual, called neap tides.

How did Apollo 11 get to the Moon?

In July 1969, three astronauts were launched on a huge Saturn V rocket. This carried them, inside a small spacecraft, into space, then on to the Moon.

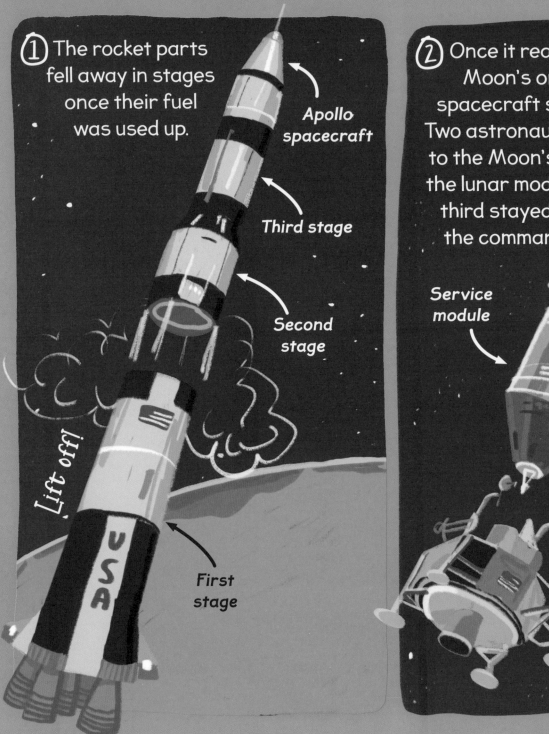

① The rocket parts fell away in stages once their fuel was used up.

Apollo spacecraft

Third stage

Second stage

Lift off!

USA

First stage

② Once it reached the Moon's orbit, the spacecraft separated. Two astronauts travelled to the Moon's surface in the lunar module, and the third stayed in orbit in the command module.

Service module

Command module

Lunar module

③ On the Moon, the astronauts collected samples of rock and dust, carried out experiments, took photographs and installed equipment.

Neil Armstrong was the first person to step onto the Moon. After Apollo 11, there were five more missions that landed humans on the lunar surface.

④ When it was time to leave, part of the lunar module carried the astronauts back to rejoin the command module.

Part of me stayed on the Moon!

⑤ The spacecraft travelled back to Earth. Then the command module, with the astronauts inside, separated. It sped through Earth's fiery atmosphere and landed in the Pacific Ocean.

Splashdown!

Would you rather?

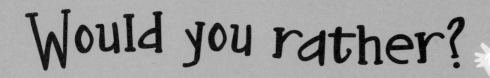

Would you rather visit the **far** side or the **near** side of the Moon?

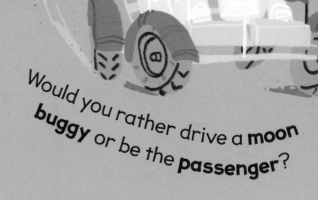

Would you rather drive a **moon buggy** or be the **passenger**?

To leave your mark on the Moon, would you rather write your **name** in the regolith or leave a **photo** of yourself?

Each Apollo mission landed in a different place on the near side.

Would you rather visit the **Apollo sites** or go somewhere **unexplored**?

Would you prefer to climb **mountains**...

Would you rather be the first person on **Mars**, or the first to go back to the **Moon**?

Which would you bring back from the Moon: a **rock** or an **Apollo souvenir**?

Did you enjoy your journey?

Would you rather find aliens on the **Moon** or be visited by aliens on **Earth**?

It's time for lunar sports! Would you rather see how far you can **throw** a ball or see how high you can **jump**?

Would you rather fly the **orbiter** round and round the Moon, or guide the **lander** down to the surface?

...or explore **craters?**

Could we live on the Moon?

We could build a Moon base that would provide us with air to breathe and a place to grow food, and protect us from the extreme temperatures.

Outside the base, we have to wear spacesuits at all times and breathe air from a tank.

Water could even be used to make rocket fuel!

Is there any water?

There is no flowing water, but there is ice, which could be melted. It is underground in rocks, and in craters near the poles. The craters are always in shadow, so the lunar water stays frozen.

The Moon doesn't have an atmosphere. It has a very thin layer of gases, called an exosphere. The mass of the exosphere is about 10 tonnes – the mass of two elephants. Earth's atmosphere has the mass of 10 quadrillion elephants!

Can I go to the Moon?

Not now – but if you become an astronaut when you grow up you might be able to. More Moon landings are planned, and we might build a lunar base to use as a stopping point on the way to Mars.

Which other planets have moons?

Mars has two but the other rocky planets, Mercury and Venus, don't have any. The gas giants, Jupiter and Saturn, and the ice giants, Uranus and Neptune, have lots – Saturn has at least 82!

Earth

> Exoplanets – planets around other stars – probably have moons, too.

> We're moonless!

Venus

Mercury

Mars

Jupiter

> Are we all the same?

No, moons can be big or small. Some are icy and others are rocky. Some moons even have volcanoes that pour out ice or lava.

Why aren't all moons round?

Saturn

Moons come in many shapes — smaller moons are often not round. Gravity makes a moon round, but only if it's big enough.

Uranus

Some asteroids (rocks in space) have moons too!

Does anything live on other moons?

We don't know. Some moons have a sea of liquid water under the surface — they might be home to tiny, simple forms of life.

Neptune

A compendium of questions

How fast does the Moon travel?

It orbits Earth at 3683 kilometres an hour. It orbits the Sun at the same time, pulled along by Earth at 107,000 kilometres an hour.

How did astronauts go to the toilet on the Moon landings?

They had to use a special bag each time, as there were no toilets on the spacecraft.

Is it colder at the Moon's poles?

In places. The Sun is always on the horizon, and because of the Moon's uneven surface, some areas are always in sunlight and some are always cold.

How do we know what the Moon is made of?

Scientists have examined rock and dust samples brought back by the Apollo missions.

Was the Moon the same when dinosaurs saw it?